BASEBALL FOR EVERYONE

STORIES FROM THE GREAT GAME

BY JANET WYMAN COLEMAN

WITH ELIZABETH V. WARREN

Harry N. Abrams, Inc., Publishers

In association with the American Folk Art Museum, New York

FOR R.C.W. AND F.W., JR.
AND SEVERAL RED SOX FANS
(THIS COULD BE THE YEAR. . . .)
AND MY THANKS TO AN ORIOLES FAN, S.V.M.
— J.W.C.

FOR FRED WILPON
AND THE NEW YORK METS——
WITH GRATEFUL THANKS FROM THE CHILDREN
OF NEW YORK
— E.V.W.

DESIGNER: Allison J. Henry
PRODUCTION MANAGER: Jonathan Lopes

Library of Congress Cataloging-in-Publication Data

Coleman, Janet Wyman.
Baseball for everyone : stories from the great game / by Janet Wyman Coleman
with Elizabeth V. Warren.
    p. cm.
Summary: An illustrated history of baseball, covering the origins of the game, some of its best-known players, and significant changes in rules and practices throughout the nineteenth and twentieth centuries.
  ISBN 0-8109-4580-0
1. Baseball—United States—History—Juvenile literature. [1.Baseball—History.] I. Warren, Elizabeth V.
II. Title.

GV867.5.C65 2003
796.357'0973—dc21

2002155971

Text copyright © Janet Wyman Coleman

Illustrations copyright © the American Folk Art Museum, New York

Published in 2003 by Harry N. Abrams, Incorporated, New York
All rights reserved. No part of the contents of this book may be reproduced without the written permission of the publisher.

Printed and bound in China

10 9 8 7 6 5 4 3 2

Harry N. Abrams, Inc.
100 Fifth Avenue
New York, N.Y. 10011
www.abramsbooks.com

Abrams is a subsidiary of

LA MARTINIÈRE
GROUPE

Bibliography

Burns, Ken. *Baseball, a Film.* PBS Home Video, 1994.

Cataneo, David. *Peanuts and Crackerjacks: A Treasury of Baseball Legends and Lore.* Nashville: Rutledge Hill Press, 1991.

Cosgrove, Benedict. *Covering the Bases: The Most Unforgettable Moments in Baseball in the Words of the Writers and Broadcasters Who Were There.* San Francisco: Chronicle Books, 1997.

Dingle, Derek T. *First in the Field: Baseball Hero Jackie Robinson.* New York: Hyperion Books for Children, 1998.

Gutelle, Andrew. *Baseball's Best: Five True Stories.* New York: Random House, 1990.

Gutman, Dan. *Baseball's Biggest Bloopers: The Games That Got Away.* New York: Viking, 1993.

Kelley, James. *Baseball.* New York: Dorling Kindersley, 2002.

Menke, Frank G. *The Encyclopedia of Sports.* New York: A. S. Barnes and Co., Inc., 1977.

National Baseball Hall of Fame. *Baseball as America: Seeing Ourselves through Our National Game.* Washington, D.C.: National Geographic, 2002.

Ritter, Lawrence S. *The Story of Baseball.* New York: Beech Tree Books, 1999.

Rosenthal, Paul. *America at Bat, Baseball Stuff and Stories.* Washington, D.C.: National Geographic, 2002.

Stewart, Mark. *Baseball: A History of the National Pastime.* New York: Franklin Watts, 1998.

Ward, Geoffrey C., and Ken Burns. *Baseball: An Illustrated History.* New York: Alfred A. Knopf, Inc., 1994.

Ward, Geoffrey C., and Ken Burns with Paul Robert Walker. *Who Invented the Game?* New York: Alfred A. Knopf, Inc., 1994.

Warren, Elizabeth V. *The Perfect Game: America Looks at Baseball.* New York: Harry N. Abrams, Inc., Publishers, in association with the American Folk Art Museum, 2003.

THE WEATHERVANE ON THE PREVIOUS PAGE IS MADE OF BASEBALL SYMBOLS. THE BATTER STANDS ON A BAT ABOVE THE FOUR CORNERS OF A BASEBALL DIAMOND, REPLACING THE DIRECTIONALS NORTH, SOUTH, EAST, AND WEST. THE BASE IS HOME PLATE. THE WEATHERVANE COULDN'T HAVE BEEN VERY USEFUL (THE WIND IS COMING FROM HOME?), SO IT WAS PROBABLY A DECORATIVE PIECE. (1930—1940)

This book is based on Elizabeth V. Warren's *The Perfect Game: America Looks at Baseball* (Harry N. Abrams, Inc., Publishers, in association with the American Folk Art Museum, 2003), and the exhibition of the same name, organized by Warren and the American Folk Art Museum, New York. On view June 17, 2003, to February 1, 2004.

Image Credits

p. 1: weathervane, The Gladstone Collection of Baseball Art, photo courtesy of Lehigh University Art Galleries, Bethlehem, Pa.; p. 3: trade figure, collection of Fred Giampietro and William Greenspon, photo by Bob Feather; p. 4: sculpture, The Gladstone Collection of Baseball Art, photo by Gavin Ashworth; p. 5: grain-painted bat collection of Paul Reiferson and Julie Spivack, photos by Gavin Ashworth; 38-inch bat, collection of Mr. and Mrs. David Hunt, photo by Michael Freeberg; p. 6: bat, collection of Mr. and Mrs. David Hunt, photo by Michael Freeberg; portrait, The Gladstone Collection of Baseball Art, photo by Sheldon Collins; p. 7: painting, collection of Neil S. Hirsch, photo by Gavin Ashworth; pp. 8–9: early photos, The Gladstone Collection of Baseball Art, photo courtesy of Lehigh University Art Galleries, Bethlehem, Pa.; balls, collection of Paul Reiferson and Julie Spivack, photos by Gavin Ashworth; p. 10: drawing, collection of and photo courtesy of Val Forgett; p. 11: lithograph, The Gladstone Collection of Baseball Art, photo by Sheldon Collins; cane, The Gladstone Collection of Baseball Art, photo courtesy of Lehigh University Art Galleries, Bethlehem, Pa.; p. 12: show figure, collection of the American Folk Art Museum, New York, promised gift of Millie and Bill Gladstone, P4.1999.1, photo by Gavin Ashworth; sled, collection of Dr. Mark W. Cooper, photo by Michael Freeberg; p. 13: box office sign, The Gladstone Collection of Baseball Art, photo by Gavin Ashworth; Boston Club sign, collection of Gary Cypres, photo by Steven Oliver; pp. 14–15: Wagner card, collection of and photo courtesy of the National Baseball Hall of Fame and Museum, Cooperstown, N.Y.; Henderson and O'Neill cards, The Gladstone Collection of Baseball Art, photo courtesy of Millie and Bill Gladstone; scorecard, The Gladstone Collection of Baseball Art, photo by Gavin Ashworth; pp. 16–17: parlor baseball game, collection of Dr. Mark W. Cooper, photo by Michael Freeberg; gameboard, collection of Tim and Charline Chambers, photo by Greg Rannels, Ferguson and Katzman Photography, Dexter, Mo., © 2002; wickets, collection of Taryn and Mark Leavitt, photo by Gavin Ashworth; bat, collection of Gary Cypres, photo by Steven Oliver; andirons, collection of Paul Reiferson and Julie Spivack, photo by Gavin Ashworth; Odd Fellows bat and ball, The Gladstone Collection of Baseball Art, photo by Gavin Ashworth; p. 18: "Tickets" bat, The Gladstone Collection of Baseball Art, photo courtesy of Lehigh University Art Galleries, Bethlehem, Pa.; Ruth photo courtesy of the National Baseball Hall of Fame and Museum, Cooperstown, N.Y.; p. 19: Yankee Stadium photo courtesy of the National Baseball Hall of Fame and Museum, Cooperstown, N.Y.; rug, collection of David Cook Fine American Art, Denver, photo by Marcia Ward; frieze, collection of Paul Reiferson and Julie Spivack, photo by Gavin Ashworth; pp. 20–21: whirligig, The Gladstone Collection of Baseball Art, photo by Sheldon Collins; carved figure of a baseball player, collection of Richard Lampert, Zaplin-Lampert Gallery, Santa Fe, N.Mex., photo by E. W. Schisler; carnival figure, The Gladstone Collection of Baseball Art, photo by Gavin Ashworth; catcher and batter, collection of and photo courtesy of Allan and Penny Katz; mechanical catcher, The Gladstone Collection of Baseball Art, photo by Sheldon Collins; pp. 22–23: beaded ball, collection of Marquette University Libraries, Milwaukee, and Buechel Lakota Memorial Museum, St. Francis, S.D., photo by Michelle D. Powers; team photos courtesy of Marquette University Libraries, Milwaukee; p. 24: Conlon photos, collection of Paul Reiferson and Julie Spivack, photos by Gavin Ashworth; p. 25: Merkle photo courtesy of the National Baseball Hall of Fame and Museum, Cooperstown, N.Y.; scoreboard, The Gladstone Collection of Baseball Art, photo by Sheldon Collins; pp. 26–27: mola, collection of Gary and Meg Smeal, photo by Gary Green, paintings, collection of Richard Merkin, photos by Gavin Ashworth; banner, collection of Richard Merkin, photo by Gavin Ashworth; p. 28: sculpture, collection of Claudia DeMonte and Ed McGowin, photo by Jean Vong; Paige photo courtesy of the National Baseball Hall of Fame and Museum, Cooperstown, N.Y.; p. 29: top painting, The Gladstone Collection of Baseball Art, photo by Sheldon Collins; Dial painting, collection of and photo courtesy of Dolly J. Fiterman; p. 30: quilt, collection of Ethel Ewert Abrahams, photo courtesy of the Kauffman Museum, Bethel College, North Newton, Kans.; sign, collection of Don and Phyllis Randall, photo by Gavin Ashworth; p. 31: dart board, private collection, photo by Greg Rannels, Ferguson and Katzman Photography, Dexter, Mo., © 2002; pinball game, collection of Dr. Michael H. Chow, photo by Greg Rannels, Ferguson and Katzman Photography, Dexter, Mo., © 2002; p. 32: Sudduth painting, collection of Ellin and Baron Gordon, photo by Jay Paul; Robinson photo courtesy of the National Baseball Hall of Fame and Museum, Cooperstown, N.Y.; p. 33: Doyle paintings, collection of Lanford Wilson, photos by Jon Reed; p. 34: quilt, collection of Kempf Hogan, photo by Dirk Bakker; drum, The Gladstone Collection of Baseball Art, photo courtesy of Millie and Bill Gladstone; p. 35: Zeldis painting, collection of the Fenimore Art Museum, New York State Historical Association, Cooperstown, N.Y., photo by Richard Walker; p. 36: comb, The Gladstone Collection of Baseball Art, photo courtesy of Lehigh University Art Galleries, Bethlehem, Pa.; carousel decoration, The Gladstone Collection of Baseball Art, photo by Gavin Ashworth; p. 37: drawing, The Gladstone Collection of Baseball Art, photo by Gavin Ashworth; quilt, collection of the San Jose Museum of Quilts & Textiles, San Jose, Calif., photo by Gavin Ashworth; quilt, collection of Timothy and Pamela Hill, photo by Paul Primeau; Arning boy, collection of Timothy and Pamela Hill, photo by Paul Primeau; Arning baseball diamond, collection of Fred Giampietro, photo by Bob Feather; p. 39: banner, The Gladstone Collection of Baseball Art, photo by Malcolm Varon; p. 40: quilt, collection of the artist, photo by Gavin Ashworth; p. 41: tapestries, private collection, photos courtesy of American Primitive Gallery, New York; pp. 42–43: Sosnak photo courtesy of Ursula Sosnak; Mets ball, collection of Gary Green, photos by Gavin Ashworth; centennial, collection of the National Baseball Hall of Fame and Museum, Cooperstown, N.Y., photo by Milo Stewart; p. 44: Fenway Park photo courtesy of David R. Mellor; painting, collection of and photo courtesy of the Fenimore Art Museum, New York State Historical Association, Cooperstown, N.Y.; p. 45: sculpture, collection of Ellin and Baron Gordon, photo by Tom Green; p. 46: sculpture, collection of Robert A. Roth, photo by Erik Weisenburger; p. 47: painting, The Gladstone Collection of Baseball Art, photo by Gavin Ashworth; p. 48: whimsy, The Gladstone Collection of Baseball Art, photo by Gavin Ashworth; weathervane, collection of Paul Reiferson and Julie Spivack, photo by Gavin Ashworth.

CONTENTS

AMERICAN TRADE SIGNS WERE DESIGNED TO ATTRACT ATTENTION, ENTICE CUSTOMERS, AND PROVIDE INFORMATION. THIS EXAMPLE PROBABLY STOOD OUTSIDE A CIGAR STORE OR LUNCHROOM. HE WAS CARVED AND PAINTED BY AN ACCOMPLISHED BUT UNIDENTIFIED FOLK ARTIST. (CA. 1885)

4 INTRODUCTION

5 IN THE BEGINNING — BEFORE 1900

5   Bats and Balls
6   "Town Ball"
7   No More "Soaking"
8   Measuring the Heroes
9   Everyone Wants to Play

10 Baseball and the Battlefield
12 "Slide, Kelly, Slide"
13 A Profit of $1.39
14 Who's on First?
16 Signs of the Game

18 HEROES & BUMS — 1900-1930

18 The Ballplayer Who Made More Money Than the President
20 Baseball's Silent Heroes
22 Native Americans Play Ball
24 "Smile!"

25 A Bonehead Play
26 Baseball Leaves Home
28 Shadow Ball, "Satchel," and a Segregated Game

30 THE WALLS COME TUMBLING DOWN — 1930-1960

30 "A National Obsession"
32 Jackie Robinson Changes America
36 Women Get a Chance at Bat

38 Little League Is Big!
39 Sawamura Strikes Out "Beibu Rusu"

40 NEW HEROES — 1960-PRESENT

40 The Old and the New
41 Records Are Broken
42 The Worst Team Wins
44 A Metaphor for America

45 Charlie Hustle
46 Just Like the Next Kid
47 The Great Game Today
48 Baseball and Folk Art

INTRODUCTION

Two friends throw a ball back and forth. One bends down and grabs it off the ground. The other reaches up and pulls it out of the sky. They back up to test their skill. "Good throw!" they yell, and "Good catch!" This is how the game of baseball often begins, and the way it probably began more than 150 years ago.

How does an artist begin? The folk artists in this book picked up a piece of wood, paper, canvas, cotton, or metal. They thought about what to make and found subjects close to their own backyards—ball games and ball players. Folk art often begins at home, just like baseball, but the art and game can take place almost anywhere.

The people you will meet in this book shared the same passion. The artists expressed their passion for baseball in sculptures, weathervanes, signs, and quilts. The athletes expressed their love of the game when they dove for home plate or made a miraculous catch.

It's not surprising that folk artists have created so many baseball images. Their art is often inspired by local or regional cultures. The images (and the players) in this book come from the United States, but also Cuba, the Dominican Republic, and Japan. Baseball is played on vacant lots and in fancy stadiums around the world. In the beginning, it was the American game. Today, baseball is a game for everyone.

IN THE BEGINNING

BEFORE 1900

BATS AND BALLS

Before there was a game called baseball, Americans had discovered the fun of swinging a stick at a ball. In the early 1800s, children held tree limbs above their shoulders and swatted at walnuts wrapped in rags. Adults swung at balls with the same enthusiasm. Broomsticks made great bats, as did large pieces of wood called "wagon tongues," named after the part of a wagon that jutted out and held the horses' reins. If players had the skill and time, they carved and sanded pieces of ash or hickory into long, graceful bats.

THIS BALL, MADE FROM OLD MATTRESS FABRIC, WAS PROBABLY SEWN BY A PLAYER'S MOTHER. (1850–1865)

Sometimes the bats were painted with a faux (false) grain to imitate the look of expensive woods and then used as trophies of good games. Balls were also made by hand, of rags, pieces of old mattress fabric, or horsehide.

The simple equipment made it possible to play "ball" almost anywhere. Soldiers enjoyed a game at Valley Forge during the Revolutionary War, and the Indian leader Geronimo fielded a team of Apaches against the U.S. Army at Fort Sill, Oklahoma, in the late 1800s. The Apaches won.

LIKE MANY PAINTED BATS, THIS GRAIN-PAINTED ONE WAS PROBABLY MORE DECORATIVE THAN PRACTICAL. (CA. 1880)

THIS 38-INCH BAT WAS PAINTED IN THE LATE 1800S. THE EARLY RULES OF THE GAME STATED THAT BATS COULD BE "OF ANY LENGTH TO SUIT THE STRIKER." TODAY'S PROFESSIONAL BATS CANNOT BE LONGER THAN 42 INCHES, AND ARE OFTEN NOT MORE THAN 35 INCHES LONG. (1870–1880)

THIS PAINTED CHILD'S BAT IS ONLY 27 INCHES LONG. IT WAS MADE OF PINE OR POPLAR, AND UNDOUBTEDLY SWIPED AT MANY PITCHES IN THE EARLY 1900S. (1900—1910)

"TOWN BALL"

Baseball may have started in the United States, but its roots are British. In England, children played a game with a stick and ball called "rounders." Adults played a game with innings and umpires called "cricket." The colonists brought both games to America, but were soon playing variations: "old cat," "town ball," "barn ball," "burn ball," "base," and "base ball."

The most popular version of the game, "town ball," had eight to fifteen players on a side, but there could be as many as fifty scattered on the field. The "feeder" (pitcher) threw the ball underhanded. The "striker" (batter) could demand a high or low toss and then wait until dark for the desired pitch. Once the ball was hit, players tried to catch it with bare hands. Gloves were considered cowardly. A fielded ball would be thrown at the runner—a practice called "soaking," "plugging," or "burning." If he was hit, it was an out. One out, and the teams switched sides. Fans (short for "fanatics" or "fanciers") sprawled on the grass or climbed trees for a better view.

THE NAME OF THE ARTIST, THE BOY, AND THE GAME HE MIGHT HAVE PLAYED (ROUNDERS OR BASEBALL?) ARE ALL UNKNOWN. THE BALL AND BAT COULD HAVE BEEN THE BOY'S FAVORITE POSSESSIONS — OR PAINTER'S PROPS. (CA. 1844)

NO MORE "SOAKING"

In 1823, the *National Advocate*, a newspaper in New York City, printed a letter signed by "a spectator." The fan wrote, "I was last Saturday much pleased in witnessing a company of active young men playing the manly and athletic game of 'base ball' at the Retreat in Broadway." The rules of the game or how often it was played are unknown. In 1842, another group of young men gathered on a vacant lot in the same city. They played variations of "town ball," depending on how many people wanted to join the game. It was so much fun, they agreed to meet regularly. Three years later, one of the players, Alexander Joy Cartwright, decided that the group needed a name. Several of the men were volunteers at the Knickerbocker fire company, so the team became the New York Knickerbocker Base Ball Club. Cartwright and a doctor from New Hampshire, Daniel Lucius "Doc" Adams, drew up a set of rules for play and conduct.

The infield would be a diamond. First and third bases must be forty-two paces apart. If a batter missed three pitches, he was out. "Soaking," throwing the ball at the runner, was illegal, to be replaced with "tagging." Pitchers still threw underhanded, but the elbow

THIS WATERCOLOR PAINTING BY AN UNIDENTIFIED ARTIST WAS DONE AFTER KNICKERS BECAME POPULAR. THE GAME BETWEEN THE TWO AMATEUR BASEBALL CLUBS (THE LIBERTY NINE OF NEW BRUNSWICK, NEW JERSEY, AND THE BALTICS OF BROOKLYN, NEW YORK) ILLUSTRATES MANY OF THE "NEW YORK" RULES. NOTE THAT THE PITCHER IS THROWING UNDERHANDED. ALSO, THE SINGLE UMPIRE (WITH THE BLACK TOP HAT) IS STANDING NEXT TO THE BATTER, AND THE SCORER'S TABLE IS NEXT TO THE FIRST BASE LINE. (CA. 1870)

and wrist had to be straight. Members were required to pay a fine if they questioned the umpire or used "profane or improper language." At the first official "match," played on June 19, 1846, the Knickerbockers lost to the New York Nine, 23–1, in four "hands" (innings). It was an embarrassing defeat for the earliest promoters of the game, but the joy of playing and the champagne dinner that followed mattered more than the outcome.

THESE EARLY PHOTOGRAPHS WERE TAKEN OF ADULTS AND CHILDREN
(BOTH PLAYERS AND FANS) WHO SHARED A PASSION FOR BASEBALL. (CA. 1880)

MEASURING THE HEROES

One of the shortstops for the Knick-erbockers was a journalist named Henry Chadwick. He invented a scoring system and a way of measuring a player's performance called the "box score." Chadwick convinced the *New York Times* and other papers to publish these statistics. For the first time, fans could keep track of their favorite players and a team's successes (or failures) without going to the games. "Batting averages" and "earned run averages" allowed one player's performance to be compared to another's and current players to be measured against heroes of the past. Newspapers attracted more fans to the game, and baseball sold more newspapers.

EVERYONE WANTS TO PLAY

In the 1840s and 1850s, thousands of ambitious young men left their families in Europe and immigrated to New York. They took jobs as policemen, firemen, and shipbuilders, and discovered baseball. Many of the immigrants were proud to be Americans and they wanted to play the American game.

Teams evolved out of the different professions. Shipbuilders pitched to firemen. Undertakers caught fly balls hit by doctors. Schoolteachers tagged out bartenders on fields and lots around the city.

However, there was a problem with the balls. They couldn't be thrown very

WORKERS IN THE LEATHER TRADE—SHOEMAKERS AND SADDLERS —MADE SOME OF THE FINEST BASEBALLS, SEWING THE PIECES OF LEATHER TOGETHER LIKE PETALS ON A CLOSED FLOWER. (1850—1865)

THIS PIGSKIN BALL LOOKS LIKE IT WAS WELL USED. (CA. 1850—1865)

far, because they were so light. Doc Adams of the Knickerbocker Club found a saddler who taught him how to sew horsehide and stuff it with rubber cuttings. At first, Adams made the balls himself "not only for our club but for other clubs when they were organized," but soon workers in the leather trade were also producing and selling balls. By the late 1860s, demand was so great, baseballs had to be mass-produced in factories.

In 1857, the Knickerbockers and fifteen other clubs that played by the same rules created a league, the National Association of Base Ball Players. Doc Adams was the president. It was decided that baseball must continue to be an amateur game. Money would be its ruination, so the players should never be paid.

INTERESTING DATES

1858
First known baseball song is published, "The Base Ball Polka."

1859
First college baseball game is played, with eighteen men on each side. Amherst beats Williams by a score of 73–32. (105 runs in one game!)

1866
Women play on the Laurel and Abenakis baseball clubs at Vassar College.

1866
President Andrew Johnson attends a baseball game, the first president to do so.

1867
The Cincinnati Red Stockings wear knickers for the first time to give players more mobility. Fans laugh out loud.

1867
Candy Cummings, of the Brooklyn Excelsiors, throws the first curveball. He learns how to throw by tossing clamshells off the docks in Brooklyn.

DURING THE CIVIL WAR, A UNION BUGLER NAMED FRANK STEITZLER DREW A COLORED PENCIL SKETCH OF WINTER CAMP ENTITLED *CAMP OF BATTERY B. 1ST N.J. ARTILLERY*. HE DEPICTED A BALL GAME IN THE BOTTOM RIGHT CORNER. IT'S UNCLEAR WHETHER THE OUTFIELDERS ARE WAITING FOR A BALL OR STANDING GUARD AGAINST THE ENEMY. (1864)

BASEBALL AND THE BATTLEFIELD

By 1861, the National Association of Base Ball Players had sixty-two teams in many states. With the outbreak of the Civil War, men left the ballfields and enlisted in the Union and Confederate armies. Some of them must have tucked a leather ball in their packs, because games were played in prisoner-of-war camps (until inmates became too weak) and near battlefields. One competition between members of the 114th New York Division of the Union Army stationed in Louisiana ended when the Rebels shot a right fielder, captured a center fielder, and stole the only ball.

For soldiers tired of battle, baseball was an escape. For those who had played before, it was a reminder of home and a happier time. Captured soldiers drew sketches of teams or carved images of players into pieces of wood, perhaps to take their minds off the poor conditions in the prisons. When the war was finally over, the soldiers returned home and spread the game to other parts of the country.

UNION PRISONERS AT SALISBURY. N.C.

DRAWN FROM NATURE BY CAPT. MAJOR OTTO BOETTICHER

OTTO BOETTICHER, A CAPTAIN IN THE UNION ARMY (68TH NEW YORK VOLUNTEERS), WAS IMPRISONED IN SALISBURY, NORTH CAROLINA. THIS LITHOGRAPH IS BASED ON A DRAWING HE MADE THERE IN 1862. (1863)

JOHN TRACY, A UNION SOLDIER, WAS A PRISONER IN THE INFAMOUS LIBBY PRISON IN RICHMOND, VIRGINIA, WHEN HE CARVED THIS CANE IN 1865. HE CHOSE SUBJECTS THAT WERE FREE (AN EAGLE, A MERMAID, BIRDS) AND REMINDERS OF A BETTER TIME (A BASEBALL PLAYER).

1868
With the opening of the Transcontinental Railroad, Harry Wright takes his Cincinnati Red Stockings to small towns across the country.

1868
William Everett writes *Changing Base*, the first baseball book for children.

1869
For the first time, fans enjoy a seventh-inning stretch. The tradition does not become popular until 1910.

1870
Catcher Doug Allison (Cincinnati) wears a pair of buckskin mittens. It is the first time a "glove" is worn in professional baseball.

1875
The catcher's mask, or "rat trap," was probably invented by Fred W. Thayer, captain of the Harvard University Base Ball Club. The Harvard catcher, James Tyng, was the first to wear the wire mesh contraption.

1877
The International Association, the country's first minor league, is established. Teams play in cities that don't have major league ball clubs.

"SLIDE, KELLY, SLIDE"

In 1863, Ned Cuthbert, a player on the Philadelphia Keystones, ran from first to second base while a batter was still at bat. The fans burst out laughing. When the umpire objected, Cuthbert pointed out that there was no rule against it. The stolen base was born. Soon, players who could get from one base to another behind a pitcher's back not only thrilled the crowd, they became heroes. One inspired a song: "Slide, Kelly, Slide."

Michael J. "King" Kelly, a handsome Irishman with an ample mustache, played for the Chicago White Stockings and several other teams. He was a great hitter, but the fans went to the ballparks to see him

UNDOUBTEDLY, THE ARTIST WHO MADE THIS SLED HOPED IT WOULD GO AS FAST AS ITS NAMESAKE, KING KELLY. (CA. 1888)

steal bases. A teammate described how King Kelly "jumped into the air ten feet from the sack" and made a "hurricane dive." In one game, he stole six bases; during the 1887 season, he took eighty-four.

Kelly didn't worry about the rules. He was known to skip second base entirely if the umpire wasn't looking. During one long game, Kelly was standing in the outfield watching the sun go down. It was the top of the ninth inning, and Chicago was one run ahead. Suddenly, the batter hit a high fly ball. Kelly leapt into the air and pretended to make a catch. When he headed for the locker room, both teams followed. The manager asked for the ball. "It went a mile over me head," Kelly told him.

THIS FIGURE MAY BE KING KELLY, THE MOST POPULAR PLAYER OF THE 1880S. THE ARTIST, SAMUEL ANDERSON ROBB (1851–1928), WAS ALSO WELL KNOWN. HE WAS AN ACCOMPLISHED CARVER DESCENDED FROM A FAMILY OF SHIP CARVERS. ROBB GAVE THIS 6-FOOT TRADE FIGURE WHEELS SO THAT IT COULD BE ROLLED INSIDE A SHOP AT NIGHT. (CA. 1888–1903)

EARLY AMERICAN SIGNS HAD LOTS OF PICTURES, BECAUSE MANY AMERICANS COULDN'T READ ENGLISH. AS THE PUBLIC BECAME MORE LITERATE, THE SIGN PAINTERS USED FEWER SYMBOLS. THEO. I. JOSEPHS, PROBABLY A PRUSSIAN IMMIGRANT, CREATED THIS BOX OFFICE SIGN. FOR THOSE WHO COULDN'T READ, THERE WERE TWO RECOGNIZABLE SYMBOLS IN THE MIDDLE OF THE SECOND LETTER "O." (CA. 1890)

A PROFIT OF $1.39

In 1869, Harry Wright, the manager of the Cincinnati Red Stockings, decided to charge admission to games and pay his players. (His younger brother, George, the shortstop, received the highest salary.) The team would finish the year with sixty-five wins, no losses, and a profit of $1.39. It was the beginning of professional baseball.

Two years later, nine teams from the New York Knickerbockers' league got together and established the National Association of Professional Base Ball Players, but the league didn't last. William Hulbert, the owner of the Chicago White Stockings, secretly bought up players and created his own organization, the National League of Professional Base Ball Clubs. The players would be paid salaries, Hulbert decreed, but owners could buy and sell them like horses. It was called "trading." In 1886, King Kelly was sold to the Boston Beaneaters for the extraordinary sum of $10,000 and paid a salary of $2,000 a year.

GROCERS OFTEN USED BASEBALL TO SELL THEIR PRODUCTS. THE BOSTON CLUB WAS PROBABLY THE BOSTON RED STOCKINGS. IN 1870, AFTER NINETY-TWO WINS, THE CINCINNATI RED STOCKINGS FACED THE BROOKLYN ATLANTICS, AND LOST. THE FANS WERE HORRIFIED AND STOPPED GOING TO THE GAMES. THAT WINTER, OWNER HARRY WRIGHT MOVED THE RED STOCKINGS EAST AND CHANGED THEIR NAME TO THE BOSTON RED STOCKINGS. (CA. 1888–1889)

SMOKE
John·A·Andrews
& Co's.
BOSTON CLUB
5 10
CIGARS
For Sale By
G.N.SHEPPARD.

IN 2000, A PRISTINE HONUS WAGNER BASEBALL CARD WAS AUCTIONED FOR $1,265,000. (1909)

WHO'S ON FIRST?

Baseball cards first appeared in the 1880s. Cigarette manufacturers who wanted to keep their soft packages from bending included a stiff piece of cardboard behind the cigarettes. The faces of baseball heroes were printed on the cardboard to help sell the product. Fans inhaled, exhaled, and collected their heroes. In the early 1900s, candy and chewing gum manufacturers decided the players' faces might help sell their products as well. Children began to collect the cards. They traded them, flipped them against walls, and taped them to their bicycle spokes to create a *flap, flap, flap* noise. Today, the Honus Wagner (Pittsburgh Pirates) card is the most valuable, worth over a million dollars. The cards are rare because very few

HARDIE HENDERSON WAS A PITCHER FOR THE BROOKLYN TROLLEY-DODGERS. IRONICALLY, HE WAS RUN OVER AND KILLED BY A TROLLEY IN 1903.

were printed. Wagner didn't like cigarettes, and he didn't want his image used to sell them.

Scorecards listing names, positions, and batting order appeared about the same time as the first baseball cards. They were decorated with illustrations and commercially printed. Fans pur-

JAMES O'NEIL
Champion Base Ball Batter

SCORECARDS LIKE THIS
ONE INCLUDED A PLAYER'S NAME
AND POSTION AND WERE UPDATED
FOR EACH GAME. HERE A FAN PEN-
CILLED IN BROOKLYN'S LEAD OF
5–0 AFTER THE SIXTH INNING. ON
THE REVERSE SIDE, AN EMBARRASS-
ED PLAYER HEADS TO THE BENCH
AFTER THREE STRIKES.

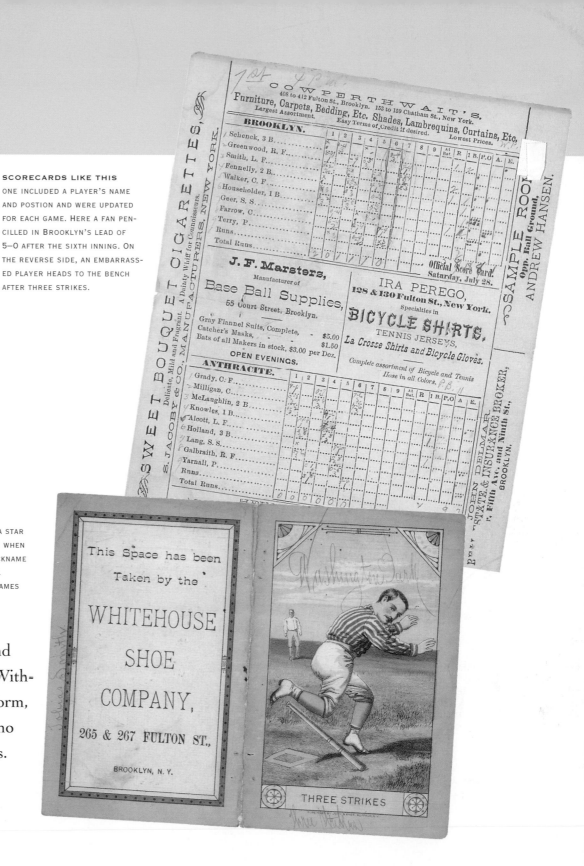

chased them for pennies at each game and penciled in strikeouts, walks, and runs. Without names or numbers on a player's uniform, or an announcer at the game, there was no other way of keeping track of the players. As the saying goes, "You can't tell the players without a scorecard."

MANY OF THE OLD RULES OF BASEBALL ARE ILLUSTRATED IN THIS PARLOR BASEBALL GAME (WITH ITS U.S. PATENT PAPERS), PRODUCED BY EDWARD B. PEIRCE OF LOWELL, MASSACHUSETTS. FOR EXAMPLE, IF A BALL BOUNCED FAIR THEN WENT FOUL BEFORE FIRST OR THIRD BASE, IT WAS IN PLAY, AND IF A CATCHER CAUGHT A FOUL BALL AFTER IT BOUNCED, IT WAS CONSIDERED AN OUT. (1878)

SIGNS OF THE GAME

By the turn of the century, baseball was so popular that fans and players found ways of enjoying it when they couldn't get to the ballpark. They played board games like Parlor Base Ball when it rained and croquet with wickets shaped like ballplayers when it didn't. Artists carved and painted "trophy bats" to commemorate a team's wins and assembled balls and bats to create advertising displays for sporting goods stores. Ballplayers even appeared as andirons for holding logs in a fireplace. Signs of the "national pastime" were everywhere.

THIS GAME WAS PROBABLY PLAYED WITH A ROLL OF THE DICE. A PLAYER (OR CHECKER) MOVED AROUND THE BASES. (THERE IS A CHECKERBOARD ON THE OTHER SIDE.) (CA. 1880S)

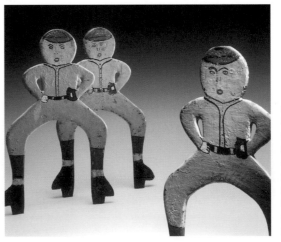

AN UNIDENTIFIED PENNSYLVANIA ARTIST CREATED THESE WROUGHT-IRON CROQUET WICKETS JUST AFTER THE TURN OF THE CENTURY. THE OBJECT OF THE GAME WAS TO HIT THE BALL BETWEEN THE PLAYERS' LEGS. OF COURSE, PLAYERS HATE TO HAVE A BALL ROLL BETWEEN THEIR LEGS, AS YOU CAN TELL BY THEIR HORRIFIED EXPRESSIONS. (CA. 1910)

THIS PAINTED TROPHY BAT IS 5 FEET LONG! IT PROBABLY COMMEMORATES THE THIRTY-SEVEN WINS OF A TEAM FROM NASHUA, NEW HAMPSHIRE. (CA. 1860–1870)

THESE ANDIRONS OF A BATTER AND PITCHER STARING AT EACH OTHER WERE PROBABLY USED JUST FOR DECORATION, JUDGING FROM THE LACK OF WEAR ON THE "DOG LEGS" (THE IRON LEGS THAT WOULD HAVE HELD BURNING LOGS). THE PIECES WERE PROBABLY SAND-CAST FROM A MOLD AND THEN PAINTED. (1890–1910)

THIS OVERSIZED BAT AND BALL MADE BY AN UNIDENTIFIED ARTIST MAY HAVE BEEN DISPLAYED IN A SPORTING GOODS STORE. THE THREE LINKS ARE THE SYMBOL OF THE INDEPENDENT ORDER OF ODD FELLOWS, A FRATERNAL ORGANIZATION SIMILAR TO THE FREEMASONS. (CA. 1910)

1878
Eight million bats
are sold in the U.S.

1882
The American Baseball
Association is established.
It is called "The Beer and
Whiskey League," because
alcohol is served. Games are
also played on Sundays, and
an admission fee of twenty-
five cents is charged.

1884
Pitchers are permitted
to pitch overhand.

1887
Batters can no longer
request high or low pitches.

1889
Batters get a "walk" after
four balls, rather than nine.

1893
The pitcher's mound is
moved back from 45 feet to
60 feet 6 inches to give the
batter more time to swing.

1894
The Compton Electrical
System produces the first
electrical scoreboard. Results
are communicated by
telegraph and pro-
jected on a ten-foot
square board.

THE BALLPLAYER WHO MADE MORE MONEY THAN THE PRESIDENT

Baseball is a game of great wins and great losses. Heroes make mistakes, and their teams lose. Rookies play better than anyone could imagine, and their teams win the World Series. In one glorious or gruesome moment, the game can create a hero or a bum. Fans argue about who was the best pitcher, hitter, or fielder, but most agree that the biggest hero was Babe Ruth.

George Herman Ruth, Jr., was called Baby, because of his baby face, then just Babe. He was a great left-handed pitcher, but an even better hitter. In the early 1900s, Ruth led the Boston Red Sox to one victory after another, including three World Series. In 1920, he was sold to the New York Yankees because the owner of the Red Sox wanted money to invest in a Broadway show. The Boston team hasn't

IT MUST HAVE BEEN QUITE A HIT. EVEN BABE RUTH LOOKS AMAZED IN THIS PHOTOGRAPH.

won a World Series since. Fans everywhere know why: it's "the curse of the Babe."

In order to accommodate all the people who wanted to see the Bambino hit a home run, the Yankees had to build a larger ballpark. Yankee Stadium, the first baseball stadium in America, opened in 1923. When the Babe hit a home run against his old team on opening day, the stadium became known as "The House That Ruth Built." The Babe set many records that would last for decades, including 60 home runs in a single season and 714 home runs during his career. He endorsed Girl Scout cookies, candy bars, cigarettes, and underwear, and made more money in 1930 than President Herbert Hoover. "Why shouldn't I?" he said. "I had a better year."

THIS AMERICAN TRADE SIGN IS A SMALL-TOWN EXAMPLE OF THE GIANT BAT THAT CURRENTLY STANDS OUTSIDE YANKEE STADIUM. (1930–1950)

THIS PHOTO OF YANKEE STADIUM WAS TAKEN ON OPENING DAY, APRIL 18, 1923. THE FIRST AMERICAN "STADIUM" SAT 62,000 FANS AND HAD "EIGHT TOILET ROOMS FOR MEN AND AS MANY FOR WOMEN."

ACCORDING TO ORAL HISTORY, A NAVAJO WEAVER CREATED THIS RUG FOR BABE RUTH HIMSELF. THE BASEBALL HERO REFUSED TO PAY FOR IT BECAUSE IT DIDN'T INCLUDE HIS NUMBER (#3) ON THE UNIFORM, SO IT WAS LATER SOLD TO AN ENGINEER WITH THE SANTA FE RAILROAD. MANY NAVAJOS USED DESIGNS THAT WERE NOT PART OF THEIR TRADITION, SUCH AS BASEBALL IMAGERY, IN ORDER TO CREATE ITEMS THAT WOULD APPEAL TO "ANGLOS," OR WHITES. (1920–1923)

YANKEE STADIUM WAS MODERNIZED IN 1973–1976 AND THIS DECORATIVE PIECE WAS SALVAGED. LOOK CLOSELY, AND YOU'LL FIND SEVERAL NEAR THE FLAG BUNTING IN THE PHOTO OF THE STADIUM ON OPENING DAY.

BASEBALL'S SILENT HEROES

Great players like the Babe inspired folk artists. An artist carved, sanded, and painted an unidentified batter with striped stockings. Many of these wooden ballplayers stood still on countertops in sporting goods stores, but a few, like those in the baseball whirligig,

THIS BASEBALL PLAYER WITH HIS HANDSOME STRIPED STOCKINGS WAS CARVED AND PAINTED BY AN UNIDENTIFIED FOLK ARTIST IN THE BEGINNING OF THE TWENTIETH CENTURY. HE IS 21½ INCHES TALL. (1910–1920)

ran around the bases.

The popularity of the game and its heroes influenced other forms of entertainment. In a traveling circus or carnival, a baseball fan paid ten cents to pitch three balls to Atta Boy Art. If done correctly, Art caught the balls and the contestant was rewarded. Another artist created a life-sized arcade ballplayer with movable arms. When a contestant threw a ball at the glove, a second ball was released, ran down a track behind the figure, and was thrown back. (It still works!) Then there are the "Strike 'em Out" Batter and Catcher. The object was to pitch a ball into the catcher's moving mitt without it being struck by the batter. However, the batter doesn't look like much of a threat with his straight legs —and missing bat.

A BREEZE BLEW THE PROPELLER OF THIS WHIRLIGIG, ACTIVATING AN INTERNAL MECHANISM THAT ROTATED A TURNTABLE, CAUSING THE BATTER TO SWING AND THE PLAYERS TO RUN AROUND THE BASES. WHIRLIGIGS WITH MOVING PARTS ARE MADE "JUST FOR FUN." (EARLY TWENTIETH CENTURY)

THIS ARCADE FIGURE IS NEARLY 6 FEET TALL AND HAS MOVABLE ARMS. (CA.1895)

H. C. EVANS & CO. OF CHICAGO ADVERTISED THEIR MECHANICAL BASEBALL CATCHER, ATTA BOY ART, AS "A NEW AND NOVEL BALL THROWING GAME THAT INSTANTLY COMMANDS THE ATTENTION OF THE PUBLIC." THE CATALOG DESCRIBED ART'S REGULATION UNIFORM AND ADDED THAT THE NEW INVENTION WAS "PURELY A GAME OF SCIENCE AND SKILL." ART MAY SEEM SMALL, BUT HE IS ACTUALLY AROUND 4-FEET TALL WITH HIS KNEES BENT. (CA. 1932)

"STRIKE-'EM-OUT" BATTER AND CATCHER WERE PATENTED IN 1929 BUT NEVER PRODUCED BECAUSE AMERICA ENTERED THE GREAT DEPRESSION, WHEN PEOPLE HAD LITTLE MONEY FOR AMUSEMENT. THE OBJECT OF THE GAME WAS TO "STRIKE 'EM OUT." THE TWO PLAYERS ARE OVER 5 FEET TALL. (1929)

square board.

1901
The Harry M. Stevens Company begins selling a steamed sausage in grandstands that would become the hot dog. In Boston, the dog is named after the ballpark: the Fenway Frank.

1903
The first World Series is played on the Huntington Avenue Grounds in Boston, also the location of the first double-decker stands.

1908
Jack Norworth writes a song about Katie Casey, who "was baseball Mad, had the fever and had it bad." Norworth had never been to a baseball game, but his "Take Me Out to the Ball Game" becomes baseball's anthem.

1908
A. G. Spalding establishes a commission to study the origins of the game. ("Our good old American game of base ball must have an American Dad," he insists.) The chairman of the commission suggests that it was his close friend Abner Doubleday who drew up the rules in Cooperstown, New York, in 1839. Though this is later proven false, 1839 becomes the official birth date of baseball, and Cooperstown the home of

THIS NATIVE AMERICAN BASEBALL, MADE AT THE ST. FRANCIS MISSION SCHOOL IN SOUTH DAKOTA, IS DECORATED WITH GLASS BEADS IN THE COLORS OFTEN USED BY THE LAKOTA (SIOUX) INDIANS. IT COULD HAVE BEEN A BASEBALL TROPHY OR USED IN A CEREMONIAL WAY. (BEFORE GLASS BEADS, BALLS WERE BEAUTIFIED WITH PORCUPINE QUILLS.) (1920–1930)

NATIVE AMERICANS PLAY BALL

In the early 1900s, baseball was introduced to Native American children in schools to "Americanize" them. The U.S. government's Indian Office promoted the game on reservations, hoping that it would take the place of traditional activities, such as dancing and rodeos. Soon, Creek Indians were playing in Oklahoma, Ojibwa Indians in Minnesota, and Lakota Sioux in South Dakota.

Native Americans who made it to the professional leagues were often called "Chief." When John "Chief" Meyers (see his photograph on page 24) and Charles "Chief" Bender walked onto the field, they were greeted with Indian war whoops and Indian war dancing in the stands. Louis "Chief" Sockalexis, a Penobscot Indian, played for the Cleveland Spiders. He had a tremendous throw, which he had developed flinging rocks

THE BASEBALL TEAM IN THIS PHOTOGRAPH WAS MADE UP OF CREEK INDIANS FROM THE BROTHERS' SCHOOL IN MUSKOGEE, OKLAHOMA. (NO DATE AVAILABLE)

across a lake at the Indian Island Reservation in Maine. Two years after his death in 1913, Cleveland fans re-named their team the "Indians" in his honor. (Today, many people object to the team's logo, Chief Wahoo, a stereotypical red-faced man with a feather.) By 1920, there were twenty Native Americans in the major leagues.

THIS IMAGE SHOWS AN OJIBWA INDIAN TEAM WITH ITS MANAGER, REV. FLORIAN LOCNIKER. THE BOYS PLAYED AT THE IMMACULATE CONCEPTION MISSION, RED LAKE RESERVATION, RED LAKE, MINNESOTA. PLAYERS WORE TEAM UNIFORMS BUT THEIR OWN CAPS. (CA. 1916—1917)

THE RIGHT HAND OF CHICAGO CUBS CATCHER JIMMY ARCHER IS "A HAND WITH A HISTORY." (CA. 1913)

ED WALSH DEMONSTRATES HIS GRIP. WALSH SAID OF HIS SPITBALL, "YOU DON'T USE A BIG GOB OF SALIVA. TWO WET FINGERS ARE ALL THAT IS NECESSARY. PERSPIRATION WILL SERVE THE SAME PURPOSE." (CA. 1913)

"CHIEF" MEYERS WAS A CATCHER FOR THE NEW YORK GIANTS FROM 1909 TO 1915. OFF-SEASON, MEYERS TOURED WITH A VAUDE-VILLE ACT AND BECAME FAMOUS FOR HIS DRAMATIC PERFORMANCE OF "CASEY AT THE BAT." (CA. 1913)

"SMILE!"

Some folk artists at the turn of the century found a new way to capture their passions: photography. Charles M. Conlon, an amateur photographer who proofread newspapers for a living, immortalized the odd-shaped little finger of a catcher for the Chicago Cubs, Jimmy Archer. "The ball fit well into the curve," Archer insisted. A Chicago White Sox pitcher, Ed Walsh, was famous for his spitball pitch, so Conlon photographed the way he gripped the ball. (Most batters hated the spitball, in part because they couldn't see it. The ball was often darkened with tobacco juice. The pitch was outlawed in 1920.)

Of course, Conlon also captured faces, including that of the Detroit Tigers' Samuel Earl "Wahoo Sam" Crawford. When he was a teenager, Crawford left Wahoo, Nebraska, with some friends in a lumber wagon. They played in one small town after another, "passing the hat" after games to pay expenses. "If we

"WAHOO SAM" CRAWFORD, FROM WAHOO, NEBRASKA, WAS A VETERAN OF THE 1913 DETROIT TIGERS. (CA. 1913)

came to a stream," he wrote, "we'd go swimming. If we came to an apple orchard, we'd fill up on apples." Conlon also photographed John "Chief" Meyers, a college-educated Native American, and many other players whose names are forgotten today.

A BONEHEAD PLAY

Baseball fans are seldom passive. They respond with cheers after a great play and name-calling after a mistake. And sometimes they become involved in the outcome of the game. On September 23, 1908, the New York Giants faced the Chicago Cubs in a race for the National League pennant. It was the bottom of the ninth inning, the score was tied, and there were two outs. The Giants were at the plate with runners on first and third.

The Giants' batter hit what appeared to be a single, and the player on third ran home to score the winning run. Fred Merkle, the Giants' runner on first, was halfway to second base when he saw hundreds of Giants fans running onto the field to celebrate the apparent victory. The nineteen-year-old rookie, making his first major league appearance, assumed the game was officially over and sprinted for the clubhouse.

A Cubs player saw that Merkle hadn't touched second base and realized that if he could get the ball and tag the base, the rookie would be "forced" out and the run wouldn't count.

A Giants third-base coach, who saw what was happening, picked up the ball and threw it into the stands. It was caught by a man in a brown bowler hat, who started to leave the ballpark. Two Cubs chased the fan through the crowd and knocked him down. The ball was relayed back to a player who tagged second base. Merkle was out!

A week later, the league president declared the game a tie. The Cubs went on to win the playoff, the pennant, and the World Series. Sportswriters and fans nicknamed the unfortunate rookie "Bonehead Merkle," and a new verb became popular. A person who "merkled" didn't show up.

DESPITE HIS BONEHEAD PLAY, FRED MERKLE HAD A SIXTEEN-YEAR CAREER IN THE MAJORS. HE LEFT BASEBALL IN 1927 AND DIDN'T ATTEND ANOTHER GAME UNTIL 1950. HE WAS ALSO A GREAT CHESS PLAYER.

A PHILADELPHIA SIGN PAINTER NAMED HOFFMAN CREATED THIS WOOD AND SLATE SCOREBOARD FOR HENRY LEISTER, OWNER OF THE LEISTER HOTEL IN HUNTINGDON, PENNSYLVANIA. A TEAM MOVED UP AND DOWN THE HOOKS DEPENDING ON ITS STANDING (OR THE MISTAKE OF A ROOKIE PLAYER!) (CA. 1892)

BASEBALL LEAVES HOME

Every fan has an opinion about the most disastrous moment in baseball—and the most exciting. On the small island of Cuba, baseball is the national game. Working from photographs, Cuban folk artist Jorge S. captured a favorite moment in Cuban baseball in paint. It was in 1922 when Armando Marsans was safe at home plate.

Baseball was introduced to Cuba in the 1800s, first by American sailors, then by Cuban students returning home from colleges in the United States. Cubans began playing regularly in the 1860s and founded a league in 1878. Thirty-three years later, two players, Armando Marsans and Rafael Almeida, were hired to play for the Cincinnati Reds. At the time, blacks were banned from the American profes-

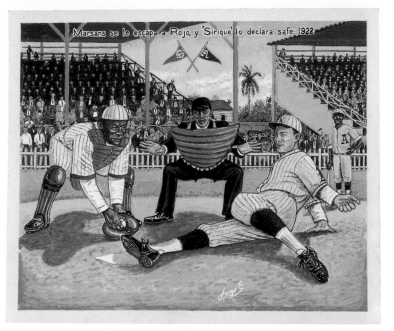

JULIO ROJO, THE CATCHER, WAS A LOCAL BOY WHO HAD A LONG CAREER IN CUBA AND MEXICO. ARMANDO MARSANS, THE RUNNER, WAS ONE OF THE FIRST CUBANS TO PLAY IN THE MAJOR LEAGUES IN AMERICA AT A TIME WHEN BLACK PLAYERS WERE BANNED. HE WAS ALLOWED ON THE TEAM BECAUSE OF HIS LIGHT SKIN. JORGE S., THE ARTIST, WORKED FROM PHOTOGRAPHS TO RE-CREATE THE GLORY DAYS OF THE CUBAN LEAGUE. (CA. 1990)

sional leagues, and the Cincinnati management worried about fan response to the skin color of the two new Cuban players. "They're as pure white as Castille soap," the management assured racist fans. Many black Americans who wanted to play professionally joined Cuban teams.

THE AMERICAN GAME OF BASEBALL HAS SPREAD TO MANY UNEXPECTED PLACES. ON AN ISLAND OFF PANAMA, CUNA INDIAN WOMEN SEW MOLAS (PANELS JOINED FRONT AND BACK TO MAKE A BLOUSE). TODAY, DESIGNS ARE OFTEN INSPIRED BY SYMBOLS OF POPULAR CULTURE. THIS NY LOGO MOLA MAY HAVE BEEN COPIED FROM A NEW YORK METS' T-SHIRT OR BASEBALL CAP. (CA. 1980–1990)

During the winter months, U.S. teams traveled to the sunny island to play teams there, and were often beaten. Cuban players spread the game to other Caribbean islands and to Latin American countries. They left home because they could often make more money elsewhere. A Cuban hero, Martin Dihigo, led the Mexican league in both hitting and pitching during one season and is a member of three baseball halls of fame: Cuban, Mexican, and American.

In the twentieth century, many children in the Dominican Republic, Puerto Rico, Venezuela, and Mexico grew up whacking balls, running for grounders, and leaping into the air for catches. Some of their children and grandchildren, like Roberto Clemente and Sammy Sosa, would become baseball heroes in America. Today, approximately one-tenth of all major league players come from the Dominican Republic.

MARTIN DIHIGO, A CUBAN STAR, IS DEPICTED HERE BY JORGE S. (CA. 1990)

1910
President William Howard Taft tosses out the first baseball on opening day of the baseball season, starting a tradition.

1918
For the first time, "The Star-Spangled Banner" is played during a World Series, as an expression of patriotism during World War I.

1919
The New York Giants beat the Philadelphia Phillies, 6–1, in the shortest big league game. It takes fifty-one minutes.

1920
Bill Wambsganss is the first to make an unassisted triple play in a World Series.

1920
The spitball is banned. However, seventeen pitchers who depend on the pitch are allowed to continue throwing it. The last legal spitball is thrown in 1934.

1921
In a 1921 court case, it is decided that fans have the right to keep foul balls.

1921
The first game — a Pirates game at Forbes Field — is broadcast live on the radio.

SHADOW BALL, "SATCHEL," AND A SEGREGATED GAME

In 1911, a newspaper called *The Sporting Life* described baseball as "a symbol of American freedom and inclusiveness." The words must have sounded unbelievable to the American blacks who were banned from playing in the major leagues. Babe Ruth was considered the "best player in the game," but who could be sure when so many talented Americans weren't allowed to compete?

Blacks formed their own teams. There were the Page Fence Giants, who rode bicycles through the streets to attract fans to games, and the All-American Black Tourists, who "paraded in top hats and swallowtail coats." In 1920, a pitcher-manager, Andrew "Rube" Foster, founded the Negro National League. Four years later, they played their own World Series.

Negro National League teams moved from town to town, taking on anyone who would play, a practice known as "barnstorming." They traveled contin-

LONNIE HOLLEY WAS BORN IN BIRMINGHAM, ALABAMA. AFTER HIS SISTER'S CHILDREN DIED IN A FIRE, HE PRAYED TO THE LORD TO DELIVER HIM FROM HIS GRIEF. "MAKE ART!" THE LORD REPLIED. HOLLEY'S WORKS ILLUSTRATE HIS PHILOSOPHY ABOUT RACIAL AND SOCIAL ISSUES. THE MESSAGE OF THE CARVED SANDSTONE *BASEBALL HAND* MAY BE THAT BLACK MEN CAN ESCAPE POVERTY AND DISCRIMINATION THROUGH THE WORLD OF BASEBALL. (1984)

SATCHEL PAIGE SHOWS OFF HIS "HESITATION PITCH." BATTERS WERE FACED WITH THE SOLE OF HIS LARGE, BLACK SHOE. THE PITCHER REFERRED TO THE MOVE AS "BLACKING OUT THE SKY."

ually, played several games a day, had few backup players, and "played hurt." They also ate and slept in "colored only" establishments or, when these weren't available, an old freight car parked on a railway siding. One team, the Indianapolis Clowns, invented a new way to entertain fans before the game. It was called "Shadow Ball": the players pitched, batted, threw with lightning speed, and made dramatic catches, all with an "invisible" ball.

One of the greatest heroes of the Negro Leagues was Leroy "Satchel" Paige. (He also played in the Dominican Republic and Cuba.) He was nicknamed "the Crane" because he was so tall and skinny. Paige sauntered to the mound, tipped backward, lifted his left foot high in the air, and "threw fire." He described several of his pitches: the bee ball (it hummed as it flew), jump ball, trouble ball, midnight rider, four-day creeper, and hesitation pitch. "I never threw an illegal pitch," he insisted. "The trouble is, once in a while I toss one that ain't been seen by this generation."

In 1947, a black man, Jackie Robinson, was finally given a chance to play on a major league team. The following year, forty-two-year-old Satchel Paige joined the Cleveland Indians. His best years were behind him, but he continued to play baseball until he was fifty-nine. When asked about his regrets, he said that he had only one: "I didn't get a chance to strike out Babe Ruth."

THIS UNDATED PAINTING OF TWO BLACK TEAMS WAS DONE BY AN UNIDENTIFIED ARTIST. THE PLAYERS HAVE NUMBERS ON THEIR SHIRTS, A PRACTICE THAT BEGAN IN THE MID-1920S, BUT THE WOMEN ARE WEARING FULL-LENGTH, BUSTLED DRESSES, A FASHION FROM MANY YEARS EARLIER.

THORNTON DIAL, SR., OF BESSEMER, ALABAMA, USED ROPE, CARPET, WIRE SCREEN, LIVE-STOCK FEED SACKING, ENAMEL, TIN, AND INDUSTRIAL SEALING COMPOUND TO CREATE *REMEMBERING THE ROAD*. THE CENTRAL FIGURE IS A BASEBALL PLAYER "TRYING TO GO FURTHER," WITH HIS MOTHER WHISPERING, "GO AHEAD." DIAL BEGAN "MAKING THINGS" WHEN HE WAS FIFTY-FIVE YEARS OLD. THIS MIXED-MEDIA IMAGE IS 7 FEET BY 10 FEET. (1992)

"A NATIONAL OBSESSION"

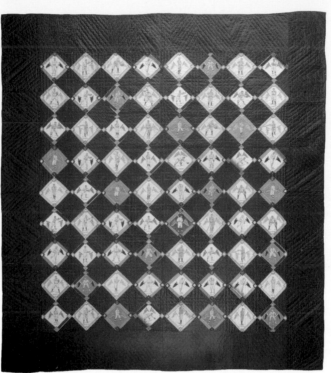

The National Hockey League was established in 1910, the National Football League in 1922, and the National Basketball League in 1937, but it was baseball that continued to be the national obsession. It was played every-where—in back alleys beneath lines of clean laundry and in the middle of the street. Batters faced pitchers in small towns and large cities, in ballparks and prison yards. Children played the game with darts and marbles. Women sewed images of baseball heroes into quilts, and everyone, or so it seemed, followed the ups and downs of a favorite team.

In the nineteenth century, news-papers filled with batting aver-ages and game results introduced the excitement and joy of base-ball to a new audience. At the same time, the popularity of the game ensured the sales of millions of papers. In the twentieth century, two new technologies would change and be changed by the "national obsession."

"Going, going, gone!" announcers shouted over radios in the 1920s and 1930s. If you wanted to hear the game "live" and you couldn't get to the ball-park, you had to listen on a radio. In 1939, spectators watched a major league

CATHRINE WRIGHT OF KANSAS CITY, KANSAS, USED SEVENTY-TWO TOBACCO FLANNELS TO MAKE THIS QUILT IN 1916. TOBACCO FLAN-NELS—LIKE BASEBALL CARDS—WERE INCLUDED WITH CIGARETTE PACK-AGES TO INCREASE SALES, ESPECIALLY TO WOMEN. THE SMALL PIECES OF COTTON WERE PRINTED WITH FLAGS AND DOLLS AS WELL AS BASEBALL HEROES AND WERE DE-SIGNED TO BE USED IN SEWING PROJECTS. (1916)

THIS DOUBLE-SIDED SIGN HUNG ON A POLE AT THE SIDE OF THE ROAD IN NEW HAMP-SHIRE. PASSERSBY PROBABLY WONDERED, IS THAT THE "RED" ROLFE OF THE NEW YORK YANKEES? (IT WAS!) THEN TURNED AROUND AND STOPPED FOR GAS. (1939)

A BULL'S EYE IS A HOME RUN! IF THE PLAYER THROWS A DART AND MISSES THE CENTER, HE CAN STILL GET A TRIPLE, DOUBLE, OR SINGLE, BUT THREE STRIKES AND HE'S OUT. (1930S)

THE EARLIEST EXAMPLES OF PINBALL MACHINES, LIKE THIS ONE, WERE HANDMADE WITHOUT LEGS. THINK HOW EASY IT WOULD BE TO TILT THE MACHINE AND CONTROL THE BALL.... THIS GAME HAS AN OUTFIELD AT THE TOP AND A BASEBALL AT THE BOTTOM. THE CONTESTANT'S SCORE DEPENDS ON WHICH HOLE SWALLOWS THE MARBLE. (CA. 1930)

game on television for the first time. It was broadcast from Ebbets Field in Brooklyn. Soon, it seemed that everyone wanted a TV, but they were expensive. So crowds gathered outside of appliance stores and stared through the windows at small black-and-white televisions or got together with neighbors to see if their team could do it again....

In 1935, baseball's biggest hero retired at the age of forty. In his last game, against Pittsburgh, Babe Ruth hit three home runs. The third flew out of the ballpark, the first out-of-the-park home run in the history of Forbes Field. The fans suffered with the departure of their hero, but many talented athletes were waiting to take his place.

1933
The Goudey Gum Company sells a rectangle of pink bubble gum and a baseball card for a penny. The product is named "Big League Chewing Gum." Today, the 239-card set in perfect condition is worth $48,000.

1935
For the first time, athletes appear on a cereal box— Lou Gehrig and Mickey Cochrane.

1935
President Franklin Roosevelt throws a switch in the White House, a signal to Crosley Field in Cincinnati. The first major league night game is played under artificial lights.

1941
An organ is played in a major league ballpark for the first time (Wrigley Field, Chicago).

1943
U.S. troops play ball at seven different diamonds at Camp Marshall, Lyautey, Africa. On one fence, a sign says, YANKEE STADIUM.

JACKIE ROBINSON CHANGES AMERICA

JIMMY LEE SUDDUTH (B. 1910), AN ALABAMA FOLK ARTIST, USES "SWEET MUD" TO CREATE HIS PORTRAITS. THE ARTIST START- ED PAINTING WITH MUD WHEN HE WAS THREE YEARS OLD. HE NOTICED THAT RAIN WASHED IT AWAY UNLESS HE ADDED MOLASSES. SUDDUTH CLAIMS TO HAVE DISCOVERED THIRTY- SIX DIFFERENT SHADES OF MUD. AS HE GOT OLDER, HE ADDED PAINTS TO CREATE COLOR. THE TINES OF A FORK PRODUCE THE THIN LINES. THIS IS A PORTRAIT OF JACKIE ROBINSON. (1989–1990)

On a hot summer day in 1945, Branch Rickey, the president of the Brooklyn Dodgers, met with a proud college-educated player from the Negro Leagues. Jackie Robinson was the son of a sharecropper and grandson of a slave. Although "free" blacks had played on the New York Knickerbocker Club before the Civil War, later team owners had agreed to keep them out of major league baseball. In the mid-1940s, the military services, hotels, restaurants, and public transportation were all segregated. White children went to white schools on buses with other white children. Black students went elsewhere. "For Whites Only" and "For Colored Only" signs restricted use of water fountains and bathrooms. How- ever, Branch Rickey felt that integration would be good for the country, for base- ball, and for the Dodgers. He also be- lieved, "it [was] a point of fairness."

WHEN JACKIE ROBINSON FIRST MET THE GENERAL MANAGER OF THE DODGERS, HE ASKED, "MR. RICKEY, DO YOU WANT A BALLPLAYER WHO'S AFRAID TO FIGHT BACK?" RICKEY REPLIED, "I WANT A BALLPLAY- ER WITH GUTS ENOUGH NOT TO FIGHT BACK."

Rickey invited Robinson to play for the Dodgers but warned him that white fans didn't want baseball integrated. "They'll taunt you and goad you…. They'll do anything to make you react."

JACKIE ROBINSON IN THE OUTFIELD WAS PAINTED BY SAM DOYLE
(1906–1985). THE ARTIST LIVED HIS WHOLE LIFE ON ST. HELENA ISLAND,
OFF THE COAST OF SOUTH CAROLINA. MANY LOCAL PEOPLE IN THE ISOLAT-
ED COMMUNITY NURTURE THEIR AFRICAN ROOTS AND SPEAK THE NATIVE
GULLAH DIALECT. DOYLE'S COLORFUL PORTRAITS ARE OFTEN OF ST.
HELENA RESIDENTS AND RELIGIOUS AND SPORTS SUBJECTS. (1978–1981)

DOYLE PAINTED THIS APPROXIMATELY 4-BY-3-FOOT IMAGE IN ENAMEL
ON ROOFING TIN AND CALLED IT JACKIE ROBINSON STEALING HOME. WHEN
THE BLACK HERO DIED, IN 1972, REVEREND JESSE JACKSON SAID, "JACKIE
ROBINSON STOLE HOME AND HE'S SAFE." (1978–1981)

Rickey explained that if Robinson lost his temper, this would seem like proof to many that blacks shouldn't be in the major leagues. He made Robinson prom-ise not to fight back for three years. "If you do what I say," the Dodgers' general manager said, "there will be more and more black players in baseball."

1948

Negro National League, one of the professional leagues of black players, disbands.

1950

The strike zone is nar-rowed from the area between the shoulders and the knees to the area between the armpits and the top of the knees.

1951

The first and only midget, or little person, plays in the major leagues. To draw fans to the game, owner and manager of the St. Louis Browns, Bill Veeck, sends Eddie Gaedel (who is 3 feet, 7 inches tall) up to bat. The Detroit pitcher is unable to throw a ball through Eddie's 1½ inch strike zone, so the player advances to first base. (The Browns lose the game 6–2.)

1951

Bobby Thompson's ninth-inning home run wins the pennant for the New York Giants (over the Brooklyn Dodgers) and becomes known as "The Shot Heard Round the World."

YVONNE WELLS, A SCHOOLTEACHER IN TUSCALOOSA, ALABAMA, EXPRESSES HER VIEWS ON SOCIAL AND POLITICAL ISSUES IN FABRIC. THE QUILT ARTIST COMMEMORATED THE FIFTIETH ANNIVERSARY OF ROBINSON'S FIRST MAJOR LEAGUE GAME, 1947, THE YEAR HE BROKE THE COLOR BARRIER. (1997)

When Jackie Robinson put on the Dodgers' uniform and walked out onto the field, it made headlines across the country. Opposing pitchers threw at his body. Runners tried to dig their spikes into his legs as they slid toward him. Teammates made racist remarks and people in the stands yelled, "Nigger." Letters arrived at the ballpark threatening to shoot the black player, his wife, and child. The manager of the Philadelphia Phillies threatened his players with "a $5,000 fine for anyone who *didn't* go after Robinson" and shoved a black cat onto the field when Robinson came to bat.

Robinson ignored the threats and played great baseball. He hit home runs

THE DODGERS' DRUM WAS PLAYED BY ONE OF A BAND OF AMATEUR MUSICIANS WHO PERFORMED DURING DODGER BALL GAMES. TO THE DELIGHT OF FANS, THE BAND LIKED TO MANGLE TUNES. THEY ALSO PLAYED "THREE BLIND MICE" WHEN THE UMPIRE MADE A QUESTIONABLE CALL AND "THE WORMS CRAWL IN AND THE WORMS CRAWL OUT" WHEN OPPOSING PITCHERS LEFT THE MOUND. (CA. 1950)

out of the park and inspired a song, "Did You See Jackie Robinson Hit That Ball?" He was aggressive and unpredictable, taking long leads off bases and stealing home plate.

Robinson would help his team win six pennants in ten years and its first and only World Series victory. It was the "Golden Era of the Brooklyn Dodgers."

Robinson kept his promise to Branch Rickey, but after three years, he spoke out. He protested when black players were not allowed to stay in a hotel with their white teammates, forcing the hotel to back down. He was criticized in the press, and he responded, "I'm not concerned with your liking or disliking me…. All I ask is that you respect me as a human being."

Robinson's performance on and off the field helped produce social change in America. By the end of the 1947 season, Rickey had hired sixteen more players from the Negro Leagues. Other baseball owners did the same. (Ironically, Robinson's success actually contributed to the end of the Negro Leagues. Fans followed their heroes to the majors.) Soon there were black players in basketball and football. Fifty years after his first game, Robinson's number, "42," was permanently retired from all major league baseball teams to honor the great man and player.

JACKIE ROBINSON WASN'T THE ONLY PLAYER TO FACE DISCRIMINATION. HANK GREENBERG (DETROIT TIGERS), THE FIRST JEWISH STAR IN THE BIG LEAGUES, FACED ANTI-SEMITISM FROM PLAYERS AND FANS. IT WAS THE 1930S AND THE LEADER OF THE GERMAN PEOPLE, ADOLF HITLER, WAS PROMOTING HATRED OF THE JEWS. "AS TIME WENT BY I CAME TO FEEL THAT IF I, AS A JEW, HIT A HOME RUN, I WAS HITTING ONE AGAINST HITLER," GREENBERG SAID. THE ARTIST, MALCAH ZELDIS, INCLUDED HERSELF IN THIS PAINTING. SHE IS THE GIRL SEATED ON THE FRONT PORCH LISTENING TO A TIGERS GAME ON THE RADIO. (1991)

WOMEN GET A CHANCE AT BAT

THIS CAROUSEL BOARD CAME FROM THE ALGONAC ISLAND PARK IN ST. CLAIR, MICHIGAN. THE BOARDS ENCLOSED THE MACHINERY IN THE CENTER OF THE CAROUSEL. THE FEMALE PITCHER IS SURROUNDED BY ARTIFICIAL JEWELS. (CA. 1915)

THIS HAIR COMB WAS MEANT TO BE WORN BY A FEMALE FAN OF THE GAME. IT FEATURES TWO PITCHERS AND TWO RUNNERS SLIDING INTO BASE. WOMEN WERE WELCOMED IN THE STANDS TO CURB THE ROWDINESS OF THE CROWD. (CA. 1870S)

Female athletes who wanted to play baseball also faced discrimination. When they first tried—at Vassar College in 1866—they played in long skirts and high-top leather shoes. The skirts were useful for trapping ground balls but had to be hiked up when a player ran the bases. It wasn't long before a Vassar student was hurt, and it was decided that the "violent" sport rather than the skirt was to blame. If women were interested in baseball, they could watch from the stands! In the 1880s, two Springfield, Illinois, teams, the Blondes and the Brunettes, barnstormed as a novelty act but played just four games. Public disgust with the "revolting exhibition of impropriety" forced them to disband.

A few years later, teams of "bloomer girls" were far more popular.

In the 1880s, Amelia Bloomer, a suffragette (a campaigner for women's right to vote), invented short, blousy "Turkish" trousers that made it easier for women to move. At first, the "bloomers" were hidden under skirts, but soon they replaced the heavy outer garments. Before long, "bloomer girls" were traveling the country playing on both all-female and co-ed teams. One star, Alta Weiss, pitched fastballs (and spitballs, though she hated to admit it) on a men's semiprofessional team. By the 1930s, many women played semiprofessional softball, but in the next decade, they would have the chance to play professional hardball as fiercely as men.

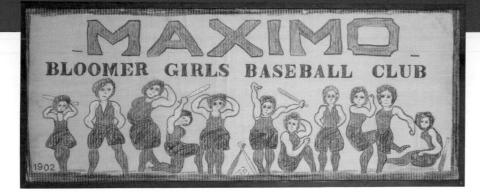

With the outbreak of World War II, many major league players went into the military service and were shipped overseas. Their positions were filled with the best players available from the minor leagues. The attendance at minor league games fell off, and fans began to look for something more exciting. In 1943, a chewing gum magnate, Philip K. Wrigley, started the All-American Girls Professional Baseball League. To attract crowds, he dressed the players in short skirts and required the "Queens of Swat" to wear lipstick on the field and high heels off. He dictated, "Femininity is the keynote of our league" and hired a cosmetics firm to teach the women charm.

The teams had names like the Fort Wayne Daisies and the Kalamazoo Lassies and players called Pepper and Jeep. They stole bases and slid into home plate, scraping their bare thighs in a cloud of dirt and pebbles. In their best year, the league attracted a million fans, but when the war was over, the major league players came home and attendance fell off. Today, women can play at the college level and in a few nonprofessional leagues, but there are no professional teams for talented players. A 1974 court decision gave girls the opportunity to play in the Little League. Perhaps a few of today's Little Leaguers will one day start a professional league of their own.

THIS QUILT WAS PROBABLY A FUND-RAISING OR FRIENDSHIP QUILT FOR A WOMEN'S SOFTBALL LEAGUE OR TEAM IN NEBRASKA. IT CONTAINS MORE THAN SEVENTY NAMES—MANY FROM THE IWANSKI FAMILY—AND OFTEN THE PLAYER'S POSITION. THE WORDS "KETTEN BALL" ARE ALSO EMBROIDERED ON THE QUILT, BUT THE MEANING IS UNKNOWN. (1930S)

LITTLE LEAGUE IS BIG!

In 1938, a man named Carl Stotz gathered a few neighborhood boys together in Williamsport, Pennsylvania, and explained the rules of baseball. The next year, he founded the Little League. The first three teams were named after the sponsors who paid thirty dollars for the uniforms: Lycoming Dairy, Lundy Lumber, and Jumbo Pretzel.

THIS **ABSTRACT IMAGE** OF A BASEBALL DIAMOND WAS DONE IN CRAYPAS BY EDDIE ARNING (1898–1993). FOR MOST OF HIS LIFE, ARNING LIVED IN A MENTAL INSTITUTION. AT THE AGE OF SIXTY-SIX, HE BEGAN TO DRAW WITH CRAYONS. HIS SPARE, ELEGANT DESIGNS WERE OFTEN INSPIRED BY MAGAZINES AND NEWSPAPERS. WHEN ARNING WAS SEVENTY-FIVE, HE MOVED IN WITH HIS SISTER AND STOPPED DRAWING. (CA. 1965)

Two years later, the league spread to New Jersey and had its first World Series. Today, there are over seven thousand leagues playing hardball and softball in more than one hundred countries. Little League is particularly popular in the Far East and Pacific Rim. Since 1969, Taiwan has won sixteen Little League World Series, while American teams have won ten.

BOY CATCHING A BASEBALL WAS ALSO DONE BY ARNING. THE BOY APPEARS TO BE LEAPING IN THE BLUE SKY. (1969–1972)

SAWAMURA STRIKES OUT "BEIBU RUSU"

Horace Wilson, an American professor teaching in Tokyo, is credited with introducing baseball to Japan in 1873. A few years later, college teams from the United States began to tour the country. They challenged Japanese college teams and won. In 1896, a Japanese nine beat a team of American residents, a victory that thrilled the Japanese. By 1905, college baseball was Japan's most popular sport.

Teams from the Negro Leagues toured Japan in 1927, and seven years later, a white all-star team made the trip as well. They won most of their games easily, but one game would become famous around the world. An eighteen-year-old pitcher,

SILK BANNERS WERE AWARDED SEMIANNUALLY TO WINNERS OF COMPANY BASEBALL CHAMPIONSHIPS IN CHONG KUO, TSINGTAO PROVINCE (PART OF JAPANESE-OCCUPIED CHINA). THE TOURNAMENTS WERE SPONSORED BY THE LOCAL HARDWARE STORE. THE LEGENDS ON THE STREAMERS TELL THE STORY: IN 1941, THE WINNERS WERE THE TSINGTAO RUBBER COMPANY AND IN 1942, THE FUJI BOSEKI (TEXTILE) COMPANY. TODAY, TWENTY MILLION JAPANESE FANS FOLLOW THE ACCOMPLISHMENTS AND FAILURES OF TWELVE TEAMS IN THE CENTRAL AND PACIFIC LEAGUES.

Eliji Sawamura, stepped onto the mound and struck out four great American heroes in a row, including a man the Japanese called "Beibu Rusu" (Babe Ruth).

1954
Willie Mays makes "the most famous catch of all time" in the opening game of the 1954 World Series. It's the eighth inning, the score is tied, and two men are on base. Cleveland's Vic Wertz hits the ball 460 feet to center field. Running straight toward the wall, Mays catches the ball with his back to the plate. "Had it all the way," he tells a teammate.

1956
Don Larsen, of the New York Yankees, pitches the only perfect game in a World Series, to catcher Yogi Berra.

1957
Major league players are required to wear batting helmets. (Pitches that hit them in the head are called "beanballs.")

1959
Harvey Haddix of the Pittsburgh Pirates pitches twelve perfect innings, retiring thirty-six batters in a row. Few people have pitched a "perfect" game (twenty-seven up to bat, twenty-seven down in nine innings), so Haddix's accomplishment is extraordinary. Unfortunately, with a hit in the thirteenth inning, Milwaukee wins 1–0.

1960
The Negro American League disbands.

THE OLD AND THE NEW

In the 1960s, many aging ballparks were replaced with big stadiums, some with domed roofs. Owners moved teams across the country to increase profits, leaving desolate fans behind. Large corporations bought up teams for huge sums, players demanded and received higher salaries, and ticket prices began to climb. The game that had been played for fun in a vacant lot became more clearly a multi-million-dollar business.

In 1960, one of the greatest hitters in baseball came up to bat for the last time. Ted Williams, nicknamed "The Splinter," had been cheered by Red Sox fans when he played well and booed when he didn't. He complained that the fans and the press were too critical. He was forty years old when he swung at his final pitch and hit it out of Fenway Park. The crowd exploded, yelling his name as he circled the bases. Williams refused to acknowledge the cheers. The author John Updike, who was in the stands, wrote, "Gods do not answer letters." The next summer, fans turned their attention to two new "gods."

CLARA SCHMITT ROTHMEIER, A MISSOURI QUILTMAKER AND PROFESSIONAL SOFTBALL PLAYER, SEWED *MY FAVORITE BASEBALL STARS QUILT*. SHE DREW PICTURES OF PLAYERS, TRACED THEM ONTO FABRIC, THEN APPLIQUÉD AND EMBROIDERED EACH ONE. ROTHMEIER SENT THE IMAGES TO THE PLAYERS AND ASKED FOR THEIR AUTOGRAPHS. THE FORTY-FOUR PORTRAITS THAT CAME BACK MAKE UP THIS QUILT. (THAT'S TED WILLIAMS IN HIS RED SOX UNIFORM TO THE LEFT OF CENTER.) (CA. 1954–1964)

RECORDS ARE BROKEN

In the summer of 1961, two Yankee outfielders and road-trip roommates, Mickey Mantle and Roger Maris, chased Babe Ruth's record of sixty home runs in a single season. Baseball fans around the country followed the competition. At first Mantle was ahead with twenty-three homers, but by midsummer, his roommate took the lead. The press demanded, "Are you going to beat Ruth's record?" A conflicted Maris replied, "I don't know.... I don't want to be Babe Ruth."

After fifty-four homers, Mickey Mantle's injuries forced him from the game. Suddenly, Roger Maris was the center of attention. If anyone asked, "Did he get one?" most people knew who "he" was and that "one" was a home run. Some of Ruth's fans booed when the contender came to bat. They didn't want anyone to have more success than their hero. Maris's hair began to fall out from the strain.

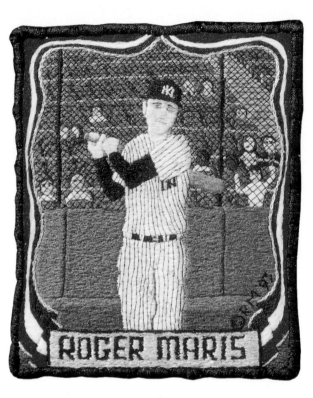

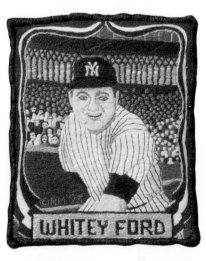

THE MINIATURE TAPESTRIES (2¾ INCHES HIGH BY 2¼ INCHES WIDE) OF THE RECORD-BREAKING YANKEE PLAYERS WERE MADE BY RAY MATERSON (B. 1954). THE ARTIST TAUGHT HIMSELF TO EMBROIDER WHILE HE WAS SERVING A FIFTEEN-YEAR PRISON SENTENCE. HE CREATED DETAILED PORTRAITS WITH THREADS UNRAVELED FROM SOCKS AND SHOELACES. THERE ARE 1,200 STITCHES PER SQUARE INCH! (1993)

In September, the Yankee batter tied the Babe's record, and in the last game of the season, he hit his sixty-first home run. Whitey Ford, the Yankee pitcher, also broke one of Babe Ruth's records—pitching 33⅔ consecutive scoreless innings, four more than baseball's greatest hero. "It was a tough year for the Babe," Ford said later.

THE WORST TEAM WINS

The year 1962 was a tough one for the Mets. The New York Metropolitans were a brand-new club playing in an outdated stadium, the Polo Grounds, with the oldest manager in baseball, Casey Stengel, age seventy-two. The team was made up of eager rookies and old veterans. Fans came to games and watched in disbelief as two runners ended up on the same base and two outfielders collided with each other and dropped the ball. "I been in this game a hundred years," Casey Stengel said, "but I see new ways to lose I never knew existed before." One player batted thirty-four times in a row without a single hit. When the catcher, "Choo Choo" Coleman, tried to catch curveballs, he looked "like a man fighting bees." Stengel asked, "Can't anybody play this game?"

The odd thing about the Mets was that the worse they played, the more the fans loved them. "Let's go, Mets!" they shouted. Huge crowds showed up at the Polo Grounds and blew their horns for players like "Marvelous Marv" Throneberry, the first baseman who often dropped balls and missed the base when he rounded second. One sign in the crowd said, "We don't want to set the world on fire—we just want to finish ninth." At the end of the first season, the team had lost 120 games (and won 40), the worst record in the twentieth century.

In 1968, the Mets did finish ninth, out

GEORGE SOSNAK (1924–1992) WAS A LITTLE LEAGUE, AMATEUR, AND MINOR LEAGUE UMPIRE. AT FIRST, HE COLLECTED AUTOGRAPHS IN HIS HOMETOWN, PITTSBURGH, THEN HE STARTED TO DRAW ON BASEBALLS. HE COVERED THE BALLS, SOME OF THEM AUTOGRAPHED, WITH INDIA INK IMAGES AND WORDS. SOSNAK PRODUCED MORE THAN 800 SPECTACULAR BALLS. THE MANAGER OF THE DETROIT TIGERS, SPARKY ANDERSON, SAID, "HE ALSO DID A GOOD JOB OF UMPIRING."

of ten teams, an accomplishment for "one of the worst teams in baseball." They had a new stadium and a new manager, but they kept losing—seven of the first ten games in 1969. Then something happened, as it often does in baseball. Sportswriters analyze great plays and great players, but no one can explain what makes a team come alive and win. In September, the Amazin' Mets took the Eastern Division title by eight games. In October, they won the World Series against the Baltimore Orioles. Suddenly, they were the "Miracle Mets"! Many fans felt that the Mets' win was as surprising as the other major event that summer: a man walking on the moon.

THE YEAR OF THE "MIRACLE METS" WAS ALSO THE OFFICIAL 100TH ANNIVERSARY OF THE BIRTH OF PROFESSIONAL BASEBALL. GEORGE SOSNAK'S *PROFESSIONAL BASEBALL CENTENNIAL, 1869–1969* INCLUDES THE LOGOS OF ALL OF THE CLUBS IN THE LEAGUE AT THAT TIME. (1969)

1962
Buck O'Neill becomes the first black coach in the major leagues (Chicago Cubs).

1964
Masanori Murakami becomes the first Japanese pitcher in the major leagues.

1965
Emmett Ashford becomes the first black umpire in the major leagues.

1969
Macmillan Baseball Encyclopedia **is the first book typeset entirely by computer.**

1972
Roberto Clemente volunteers to take supplies to victims of an earthquake in Nicaragua and is killed in a plane crash. The great hitter and right fielder for the Pittsburgh Pirates is the first Latino player to be inducted into the Hall of Fame.

1975
Frank Robinson becomes the first black manager in the majors (for the Cleveland Indians).

1976
A Chicago announcer named Harry Caray sings "Take Me Out to the Ball Game" during the seventh-inning stretch. Fans join in, and the song becomes a ritual of the game.

A METAPHOR FOR AMERICA

DAVID R. MELLOR, THE DIRECTOR OF GROUNDS AT FENWAY PARK IN BOSTON, ROLLS THE GRASS INTO WORKS OF ART. THE GRASS REQUIRES TOUCH-UPS EVERY FEW DAYS. HIS TOOLS ARE ROLLERS OF DIFFERENT WIDTHS: 21 INCHES WIDE FOR THE IN-FIELD AND 6 FEET WIDE FOR THE OUTFIELD. THE ROLLER PASSES OVER THE GRASS AND BENDS THE BLADES SO THAT THEY APPEAR TO BE DIFFERENT SHADES OF GREEN WHEN THE SUN HITS THEM. (2001)

The 1960s and 1970s were a chaotic time in America. A young president, John F. Kennedy, and a black leader, Martin Luther King, Jr., were both assassinated. There was a war in Vietnam and continual protests against this war at home. In the summer of 1974, Richard M. Nixon resigned the presidency in disgrace. Of course, the events and social issues of the time inspired artists.

Ralph Fasanella (1914–1997) was a reform-school student, gas-station attendant, truck driver, ice delivery man, union organizer, and artist. In *Night Game—Yankee Stadium*, he makes a reference to Martin Luther King, Jr., and the bad state of urban neighborhoods (represented by an abandoned gas station). In the middle is Yankee Stadium. "How can you paint American history without baseball?"

IN *NIGHT GAME—YANKEE STADIUM*, THE VIEWER CAN FEEL THE EXCITEMENT OF THE CROWD SPENDING THE NIGHT OUT UNDER THE LIGHTS. RALPH FASANELLA, THE ARTIST, WHO LIVED IN NEW YORK, SAID HIS OIL PAINTINGS ALLOWED HIM TO "EXPRESS HIS COMMITMENT TO THE WORKING CLASS." (1981)

he asked. "It wouldn't work."

Several decades later, the director of grounds at Boston's Fenway Park, David R. Mellor, was also affected by American history. He created a flag pattern in the outfield by rolling the grass. It was a quiet response to the terrorist attacks of September 11, 2001.

CHARLIE HUSTLE

One of the most controversial heroes in baseball history is Pete Rose, who played for and managed the Cincinnati Reds. When he was a little boy, his father and uncle made him bat one hundred times from the right and one hundred times from the left before bed. Rose wasn't the most skilled professional baseball player, but he ran, dove for bases, and competed in every game as if nothing else mattered. "Let the other guys go out and give 100 percent if they want. They're good," he said. "Me? I've got to give 110 percent to keep up with them." Fans called him "Charlie Hustle."

In 1978, Rose hit in forty-four consecutive games. By 1985, he had gotten more base hits (4,256) than any other player in history, including Hank Aaron. The next year, he became manager of the Reds, but in 1989, he was barred from baseball for life. Rose allegedly had a gambling addiction and was accused of

having bet money on the outcome of games. If so, was he managing the team to win the game or the bet? The commissioner of baseball, A. Bartlett Giamatti, explained why gambling could not be tolerated: Baseball, "because it is so much a part of our history as a people, and because it has such a purchase on our national soul, has an obligation to the people for whom it's played." The obligation, he felt, was to keep the game honest.

ELIJAH PIERCE (1892–1984) PRODUCED THIS 13-INCH SCULPTURE OF PETE ROSE. IT WAS MADE WHEN THE ARTIST WAS EIGHTY-NINE AND HAD BEEN CARVING FOR MORE THAN EIGHTY YEARS. (1981)

1981
Professional baseball's longest game, between the minor league Rochester Red Wings and the Pawtucket Red Sox, begins on April 18, and continues on June 23, lasting 33 innings.

1981
Sadaharu Oh retires after hitting 868 home runs for Japan's Yomiuri Giants.

1986
A Mets fan parachutes into Fenway Park during the first inning of a World Series games. His banner says, "Let's Go, Mets," and his team wins the game.

1987
Mark McGwire hits more home runs (49) than any other rookie in history.

1991
A 44-year-old Rangers pitcher named Nolan Ryan pitches his seventh no-hitter, against the Toronto Blue Jays. The previous record was four no-hitters.

1992
The Toronto Blue Jays win the World Series, the first non-U.S. team to do so.

JUST LIKE THE NEXT KID

Although Pete Rose got 485 more base hits than Hank Aaron, the right fielder for the Atlanta Braves, Aaron is the home run king. During the summer of 1973, Aaron's home run total approached Babe Ruth's record of 714. Once again, there were fans who didn't want a legend's record broken, especially by a black man. Aaron received death threats that were as vicious as those endured by Jackie Robinson. In the last game of the season, Aaron was one run short of the Babe's record. He swung and popped out. When he re- turned to right field, the fans behind him stood up and applauded. Before long, 40,000 people were on their feet clapping and cheering. "All I'd done was pop up to second base," Aaron recalled. The standing ovation lasted five minutes.

At the beginning of the next season, Hank Aaron walked up to bat for the first time and hit a home run. Four days later, he hit another. When he left base- ball, he had hit 755 home runs. "On the field… your skin color or how much money you have doesn't matter," Aaron wrote. "When you play baseball, you get a turn at bat just like the next kid."

REVEREND JOSEPHUS FARMER A STREET PREACHER WHOSE FATHER AND GRANDFATHER WERE SLAVES, CARVED AND PAINTED THIS WOODEN TRIBUTE TO HANK AARON. THE PLAYER WAITS IN THE ON-DECK CIRCLE FOR HIS TURN AT BAT. FARMER BEGAN MAKING WOODEN SCULPTURES, MANY WITH RELIGIOUS AND HISTORICAL THEMES, WHEN HE RETIRED FROM HIS JOB AS A HOTEL PORTER. (1974)

THE GREAT GAME TODAY

Today, baseball continues to produce heroes. Sammy Sosa supported his mother and five siblings by shining shoes in the Dominican Republic. A few years later (1998), the Chicago Cubs outfielder hit sixty-six home runs—six more than Babe Ruth's record. The same year, Mark McGwire, of the St. Louis Cardinals, hit seventy. Barry Bonds, of the San Francisco Giants, considered by many to be the best player in the game, hit seventy-three in 2001. There are baseball fanatics who point out that Babe Ruth played a shorter season than Bonds. If he'd had more games, he might have hit more home runs. And the ball was not as lively in the early 1900s, so it was more difficult to hit it out of the ballpark. If only the old hero could step up to the plate today....

Today, many fans take their families to minor league games. The small ballparks are a reminder of the way baseball used to be played. Hundreds of thousands of

IN *HOMAGE TO SAMMY SOSA*, DOMINICAN ARTIST FELIX LOPEZ PAINTED THE BALLPARK IN CONSUELO, SAN PEDRO DE MACORIS, WHERE SAMMY SOSA PLAYED AS A YOUNG BOY. (SAN PEDRO DE MACORIS HAS BEEN CALLED THE "PATRON SAINT OF SHORTSTOPS" BECAUSE IT HAS PRODUCED SO MANY MAJOR LEAGUE SHORTSTOPS.) "TEXAS" APPEARS ON THE OUTFIELD FENCE BECAUSE SOSA SIGNED WITH THE TEXAS RANGERS WHEN HE WAS SIXTEEN YEARS OLD. (CA. 1990)

people also play a game called Rotisserie (or Fantasy) Ball. They manage imaginary teams using the statistics of real players, which they often check on-line. Barry Bonds "plays" on a Rotisserie team. He doesn't show up, but his batting average and home runs in a game affect the outcome of Rotisserie Ball the next day.

1995
Cal Ripken of the Baltimore Orioles plays in his 2,131st consecutive game, beating Lou Gehrig's record from 1939. (Ripken hadn't missed a game since 1982.) When the achievement was announced at baseball parks across America, players and fans stood and applauded.

2000
George W. Bush is the first Little Leaguer to become President of the United States. When he was playing in 1955, his father wrote, "He has good fast hands and even seems to be able to hit a little."

2001
Roger Clemens wins his sixth Cy Young Award for the best pitching in the American League. Clemens won the awards while pitching for three different teams.

2002
Rickey Henderson of the Boston Red Sox steals his 1,403rd base, more bases than any player in history. Lou Brock, who comes in second, stole 938.

BASEBALL AND FOLK ART

The game of baseball will continue to produce great players, remarkable teams, and unbelievable games. Fans of different generations and cultures will share the excitement. In the stands and in front of television sets, they'll discuss the heroes, the bums, and the legends. "What a hit!" they'll shout. Afterward, someone may ask, "So, how does Bonds compare to the Babe?"

Baseball fans remember George Herman Ruth, Jr., but the names of many other players have been forgotten. In 1937, the photographer Charles Conlon wrote, "I could do quite a book around those hundreds of fine pictures I still possess, but, how many of the present generation would know anything about the men depicted?" Think of all the impossible catches and out-of-the-park home runs made by unknown players. Then notice how many works of art

THIS COPPER WEATHERVANE IS VERY SIMILAR TO THE ONE THAT SITS ATOP YANKEE STADIUM TODAY. IT IS AS SIMPLE AND BEAUTIFUL AS THE GAME ITSELF. (TWENTIETH CENTURY)

in this book were created by anonymous artists.

Baseball players and folk artists have more in common. Many are self-taught or shown "how to do it right" by a parent or grandparent. "Choke up on the bat," they are told, or "Make the stitches a little smaller." The materials are simple: a round ball or a square piece of cloth. As the athletes and artists work, they imagine what lies ahead. Batters picture themselves swinging for the fences. Pitchers dream of throwing fast balls, sinkers, and sliders. Artists want their art to be appreciated. (Perhaps someday it will be in a book or a museum.) In the future, there will be new heroes, and new artists inspired by them. At the moment, they're still practicing.

"BIRD-IN-CAGE" WHIMSEYS WERE OFTEN CREATED TO SHOWCASE AN ARTIST'S ABILITY. THE WHITTLER WORKS FROM ONE PIECE OF WOOD AND CARVES UNTIL AN OBJECT CAN MOVE FREELY WITHIN ITS "CAGE." ED DIXON OF LOUISVILLE, KENTUCKY, NOT ONLY FREED THE BASEBALL IN THIS WHIMSEY, HE ALSO FREED AN ALMOST LIFE-SIZED BAT. WHAT A SHOW-OFF! (CA. 1930)

48